My New
Childminder

By Jillian Powell

Photography by Chris Fairclough

WAYLAND

First published in 2011 by Wayland

Copyright © Wayland 2011

Wayland
338 Euston Road
London NW1 3BH

Wayland Australia
Level 17/207 Kent Street
Sydney, NSW 2000

Editor, Wayland: Julia Adams
Produced for Wayland by Discovery Books Ltd
Managing editor: Rachel Tisdale
Project editor: Colleen Ruck
Designer: Ian Winton
Photography: Chris Fairclough
Consultant: Helen Beale (Teacher and Library Coordinator,
Robert Le Kyng Primary School, Swindon)

The author and photographer would like to acknowledge the
following for their help in preparing this book: Jack and Phoebe
Condliffe; Amy Bowen; Sarah, Hayley and Adam Mumford; Natasha
Martin; Louis Griffiths; Evan and Rowan Prosser; Cameron Loring;
William Andrews and staff and pupils at Ludlow Infant School.

British Library Cataloguing in Publication Data
 Powell, Jillian.
  My new childminder.
  1. Family day care--Pictorial works--Juvenile literature.
  I. Title
  362.7'12-dc22

ISBN: 978 0 7502 6288 0

Printed in China

Wayland is a division of Hachette Children's Books, an Hachette UK company.
www.hachette.co.uk

Contents

My family

My name is Jack. I live with my Mum and Dad and my little sister Katie.

When Mum and Dad go to work Sarah will look after us.

Sarah is our new **childminder**.

In the morning,
Mum gets
our breakfast
before she
goes to work.

My new childminder

After breakfast Mum takes us to Sarah's house. It is a short walk from home.

This is my first time at Sarah's house. I feel a bit sad when Mum leaves.

Sarah looks after other children, too.
She takes us all to school. Sarah looks
after Katie when I am in school.

After school

After school, Sarah comes to pick me up. Mum and Dad used to collect me. I miss them, but it is nice to see Katie.

Katie has been playing with Evan and Rowan today. Sarah is their childminder, too.

On the way back, Sarah
takes us to the park.

I play football with
Evan while Sarah
pushes Katie and
Rowan on the swings.

At the park

Sarah also looks after William when he finishes school. She watches us take turns to go down the **slide**.

It's fun going down as fast as you can!

After the park, we all go back to Sarah's house.

Playing indoors

When we get back, Sarah shows me her pet cat. He is called Tom.

I don't have a pet at home, so I like playing with Tom.

There are lots of games we can play at Sarah's house.

William and I play a board game called Wee Little Piggies. I like playing board games.

13

Arts and crafts

Next, Sarah shows us how to make paper flowers. William and I choose different colours for our flowers.

I am going to give my paper flowers to Mum when she picks me up.

15

Dinner time

Now it is time for dinner. Sarah makes us some **sandwiches**.

William is very hungry. He has been playing football at school.

It is strange not seeing Mum after school, but it is fun at Sarah's house.

Sarah shows me how to make fruit **kebabs**. They are really tasty!

17

Having fun

Sarah has lots of toys at her house.
We play shops together.

I go and play in the garden with William until Mum picks me up. We like playing on the elephant **seesaw**.

We try to make it go faster!

Home with Mum

When Mum
is finished
at work, she
comes to pick
me up from
Sarah's house.

Mum loves
the flowers
I made her!

When we get home, I tell Mum all about my day at school and what we did at Sarah's house. Then we read my favourite book together.

Glossary

childminder someone whose job is to look after children.

kebabs a meal made by pushing sticks through food.

sandwiches slices of bread with a filling between them.

seesaw a play seat that goes up and down when two people ride it.

slide a frame that you can climb up one side then slide down the other on your bottom.

Further information

Books

Popcorn: Good Food: Fruit by Julia Adams (Wayland, 2010)

Lets do Art: Having Fun with Paper by Sarah Medina (Wayland, 2007)

Websites

www.bbc.co.uk/cbbc/bugbears
This interactive website provides support and advice for children facing new situations, such as 'making new friends'.

www.cyh.com
The Kids' Health section of this website includes helpful facts and information on topics such as family, school and feelings.

Things to do

Speaking and listening/role play
Make up a play with your friends or childminder. Choose what character you want to be and get your friend or childminder to choose too. You could be a pirate or a superhero, a fairy or a princess.

Art
Make some finger paintings. Ask your childminder to get some paints and paper and to help you. Dip your finger in the paint and then press down on the paper. You will see your colourful fingerprint. Try making some flowers and animals with your fingerprints.

Writing
Make a list of some of the things you like to do with your childminder. Next make a list of some things you would like to do. This could be a trip to the zoo, a picnic or a nature walk.

Index

My New

Contents of titles in series:

Childminder
978 0 7502 6288 0

My family
My new childminder
After school
At the park
Playing indoors
Arts and crafts
Dinner time
Having fun
Home with Mum

Friend
978 0 7502 6286 6

My home
Neighbours
Classmates
Visiting Emily
Playing together
Not friends?
Together again
Emily's birthday
The party

Sister
978 0 7502 6285 9

My family
Shopping for baby
Getting ready
Mum goes to hospital
My sister Holly
Helping out
At home with my sister
Playtime
Bath and bedtime

Dad
978 0 7502 6287 3

My family
Moving in
Changes
Helping us
Kevin's son
Weekends
Family arguments
Having fun
My step-family

School
978 0 7502 6284 2

My first day at school
My class
Assembly
Paint and play
Snack time
Reading and writing
Lunch
Circle time
Going home

WAYLAND